Tidy up!

Julia Lawson

Photographs by
Peter Millard

Evans Brothers Limited

I can't find my teddy. Can you see it?

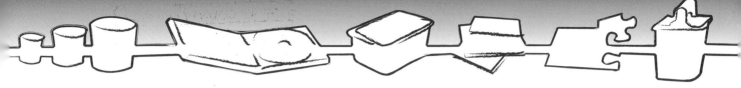

What a mess! I'll have to tidy up. I think I need some help.

We're sorting out the toys. We'll put them into their boxes.

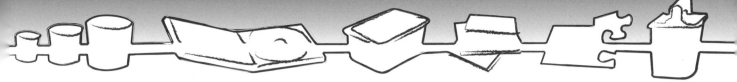

What shall I write on this label?

JIGSAWS

Will there be enough space for all these CDs on the rack?

There's plenty of room for the videos.

Now for the books. Some will fit in the baskets.

Others are too big, but will they fit on the shelves?

Can you play this matching game? You need some containers of different sizes and some toys, books and games. You have to find a box that's the right size for each toy - not too big and not too small!

We can put small toys into a box so that they don't get lost.

We can stack these large bricks.

The cups fit one inside the other.

Tidy Up Song
(to the tune of 'Frère Jacques')
Are you helping? Are you helping?
Pick up toys, pick up toys.
Let's all help each other, let's all
help each other.
Girls and boys, girls and boys.

It's easy to fold this away.

Rolling the mat is easier with two of us!

There you are,
Teddy!
Your clothes
need a wash
before you
can go away.

Little Teddy lying there,
Without your clothes you look so bare.
With a rub and a scrub and a quick rinse through,
You're soon looking as good as new!

We'll need to finish the jigsaws before we can put them away.

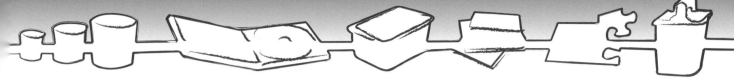

Oh no! One piece is missing! Can you see it? I'm sure it's here somewhere.

Notes and suggested activities for parents and teachers

We hope that you have enjoyed sharing this book and have tried some of the additional ideas found in the activity boxes. Other activities you may wish to try are listed here, along with a poem, some children's storybooks, a website, video and CD-Rom, which all tie in with the theme of tidying up. Have fun!

Early maths

Sorting activities are an excellent way of introducing mathematical concepts to young children. Here are some sorting games you could try:

Guess the Set! Using a collection of objects, for example farm animals, coloured beads or cars, sort them out according to a rule. The rule could be all animals with four legs, all square beads, or all red cars. The other players have to guess the rule the sorter is using. You can make this even more fun if the sorter wears a special 'sorting hat'!

Where's the Pair? Using a collection of pairs, for example socks, gloves, a knife and fork or a cup and saucer, remove one half of a pair, making sure no one is looking. Having rearranged what's left, the other players then have to work out what is missing by pairing up the remaining articles.

Make it Fit! This game is also a great problem-solving activity!
Give each child a small box and a selection of objects you would like tidied up, for example bricks, books, cassette tapes, beads, cars or pencils. The children have to put their objects into the box so that everything fits neatly, nothing falls out and the lid closes. It's harder than it looks!

How many? This is a fun variation of *Make it Fit!* Give the children a matchbox and ask them to find as many things as they can that will fit inside. You'll be amazed at how many they can squeeze in!

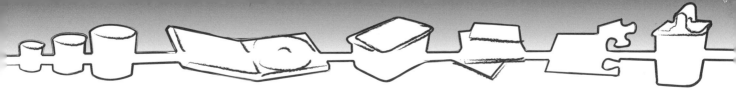

Storybooks
Tidy Titch, Pat Hutchins, Red Fox
Tidy Up Titch, Pat Hutchins, Red Fox
Tidy Up Trevor, Rob Lewis, Red Fox
The Great Tidy Up, Iona Treahy, Madcap
Kipper's Toybox, Mick Inkpen, Hodder
Tidy Your Room!, Trevor Todd,
David & Charles

Poem
Tidy Up Time
My books and toys fill all the room,
There is no space to rest,
So now it's time to tidy up,
I'll have to do my best!

I pick up all the little things,
That should be somewhere else,
And put them where they ought to be –
My toybox or my shelf.
My picture books go in a stack,
And on the shelf then back to back.
Then all my toys except my bear,
I line up and put somewhere.
All my cars and planes and bricks,

The castle, house and farm,
The doll, the puzzle, the pick-up sticks,
Go where they're out of harm.

Now my room's all tidied up,
I shout out "Come and see!"
You'll be so happy and surprised,
And so, so proud of me!

Website
www.bbc.co.uk/education/teletubbies/
playground

A number of games on this site may be
suitable and they change regularly.

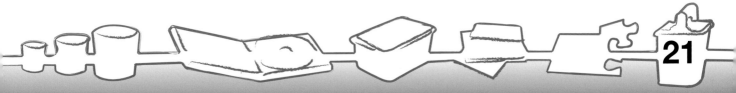

Video and CD-Rom
The Cat in the Hat (Dr Seuss)

Sesame Street: *Search and Learn
Adventures* (CD-Rom)

Index